Tap it Tad

Written by Natasha Paul

Illustrated by Amy Zhing

Collins

Tap it Tad. Tap.

tap tap tap tap

3

Pat it Tad. Pat.

pit pat pit pat

Dad taps. Dad naps.

Pat a pad. Pat.

Dad sits. Dad tips.

Tip Dad in it!

Nip it. Nip it.

Nip at a pad.

It tips. It dips.

Mad Dad tips in!

After reading

Letters and Sounds: Phase 2

Word count: 48

Focus phonemes: /s/ /a/ /t/ /p/ /i/ /n/ /m/ /d/

Curriculum links: Understanding the World

Early learning goals: Reading: read and understand simple sentences; use phonic knowledge to decode regular words and read them aloud accurately

Developing fluency

- Your child may enjoy hearing you read the book.
- Take turns to read a page of the story. Encourage your child to read the sound words on pages 3 and 5 with expression.

Phonic practice

- Point to the word **Pat** on page 4. Ask your child sound out and then blend the word. (P/a/t – Pat)
- Point to page 5 and ask them to find the word **pit** (emphasise the /i/ sound as you say the word).
- Repeat for pages 11 and 13. Point to **pad** and ask your child to sound out and blend p/a/d – pad. Can they find and read **Dad** on page 13?
- Look at the "I spy sounds" pages (14 and 15). Point to the mole and say: I spy a /m/ in mole. Challenge your child to point to and name different things they can see containing a /m/ sound. Help them to identify /m/ items, asking them to repeat the word and listen out for the /m/ sound. (e.g. *moth, magnet, mud, chameleon, comet, worm, moon*)

Extending vocabulary

- Turn to page 6 and discuss the meaning of **naps**. Ask your child what other words could be used instead. (e.g. *sleeps, dozes*)
- On page 10, discuss what is meant by **nip**. Ask your child what other words could be used instead. (e.g. *bite, eat, nibble, chomp*)